God Encounters

Securing Your Inner Healing

By Christy Lane

ISBN-13: 978-1533286253

Printed in the United States of America
First printing June 2016
Typography and cover design—Nathan R. Sewell

Table of Contents

Acknowledgements

Thank You, Jesus, for placing the desire in my spirit to write this book. You are my heart's desire, and I long to know You more. Thank You, Holy Spirit. Without Your guidance, this would have never come to fruition. Thank You, Father. You love to meet me at my greatest need.

Thank you, Russ, my dear husband. Your belief and encouragement have spurred me on. Thanks to all my dear friends who have encouraged me to run after God and fulfill all His purposes: Steven and Camilla; Randy; Larry and Linda; Lynn, Amy, Nathan, Jeffrey, Katy; and many members of Bethesda and Bethel churches.

Special thanks to Sandi for editing. I also want to thank Brian for pushing me out of the nest to go for it.

A Note From The Author

I wrote this book to hopefully help you stay on course with all that was spoken over you during your time of inner healing.

My prayer is that some of these devotionals will hit you right where you are walking at the moment. Others might be good information to tuck away for later. My purpose is to encourage you to keep your mind renewed. Your transformed mind *will prove* the perfect and acceptable will of God. Some behavioral psychologists say it takes at least 21 days to establish a new habit. There are enough thoughts here to take you through 21 days.

I was privileged to lead inner healing sessions at my church in Texas. Many excellent models are out there, and I used the Sozo model.

There were remarkable breakthroughs and revelations. I always went to each session with "fear and trembling," knowing I was not adequate. But the Godhead always showed up and beautifully met people where they were and brought His amazing transforming touch. I saw faces of torment turn to joy, wonderment, and peace. I felt atmospheres change as the presence of God filled the room with His redeeming touch. As lies fled and truth came to each spirit, laughter, tears, and freedom were released. It was truly an exceptional moment every time.

Inner healing sometimes comes in layers, as people walk in the truth they have and wait for more truth to be manifest. As I watched this in individuals, a passion was stirred to write encouragement for the journey. I wanted to offer some insight through the stories of my journey and lessons I've learned over the years. We all need someone like Barnabas to come alongside and call out the greatness in us.

I bless your spirit to receive all that God has for you in the days ahead. I am so excited about your new adventures in God! If any of these devotions have been a help, I would love to hear from you at the address in the back of the book.

Many, many blessings,
Christy

Endorsements

Brilliant, practical, powerful! Christy Lane, by being courageously vulnerable, has captured the essence of clarity, quality, and intimacy in presenting a devotional that is designed to transform daily. She will usher you into the Presence of God, where He will encounter you in intimacy and transform how you think, what you feel, and how you live your life. Christy invites you into her encounters as a doorway of invitation into your own encounters!

Lynn Strietzel, Author and Bethel Healing Rooms Leadership Team, Bethel Church, Redding CA

Christy has always demonstrated a passion for God. Her intimate relationship with the Lord has modeled for our church family how to live supernaturally natural in all seasons of life. I had the privilege of watching Christy's gentleness and wisdom with those who came for a Sozo. It was a joy to see so many set free! Her book continues her journey to help others experience more God encounters. I highly recommend this book to all who are desiring to cultivate their relationship with the Godhead-Father, Son, and Holy Spirit.

Camilla Charles, Bethesda Church/co-pastor, Lindale, Texas

Christy Lane has provided her readers with a wonderful opportunity to encounter the Lord and further the inner healing they have received through Sozo or other healing ministry. This work is a fresh breath of the wind of the Holy Spirit into the world of God encounters. Her honesty about her own journey is refreshingly transparent. I highly recommend her book to all God seekers.

Dr. Jeffrey Barsch, Author and Sozo Counselor, Bethel Church, Redding CA

Introduction: Saved, Healed, and Delivered

Your inner healing sessions most likely confronted some lies that were interfering with your relationship with God; perhaps even distorting or misrepresenting His character to you. Often these lies affect the relationships we have with others as well. It could have been a traumatic event or a series of events or behaviors that built upon one another to create the lie. Thoughts, if dwelt upon and pondered long enough, become patterns of thinking. These patterns of thought become habits, which when entrenched, become who we are and create a way of life. Lies, when broken, release the negative cycle and set you free to become whom you were created to be.

And do not be conformed to this world, but be transformed by the renewing of your mind, that you may prove what is that good and acceptable and perfect will of God.

(Romans 12:2)

Inner healing can be somewhat likened to a pool game. During my teen years, my family purchased a pool table for recreation. I learned that if I wanted the ball to go into a certain pocket, I had to hit the cue ball at a specific angle and/or speed. By learning some physics and geometry, I could move it 45 degrees from the cue ball.

It's the same way with some habitual thought patterns. They can be hit so hard, they are smacked into a different direction forever. The jolt of revelation is so startling, there is no turning back. You may have experienced this in your inner healing session(s).

Other thought patterns are like the turning of a huge ocean liner. The back rudders determine the direction of the ship. However, these rudders are small in comparison to the size of the vessel. In some areas, you may need encouragement until the ship has turned completely. In others, your small boat may get sucked into a whirlpool where the enemy tries to steal your blessings.

The large ship *begins* to turn, just much slower than a small boat. If you don't mess with the rudders, the ship eventually goes in the direction intended. *Your* rudders, God's truth spoken over you, change the direction of *your* ship.

The process has begun!

Day 1: Stewarding Your God Encounter

Has this ever happened to you? You've just had an amazing encounter with God. You've heard His voice, sensed His presence, received confirmation about direction, had a prayer swiftly answered, and even had goose bumps to top it all off. And then it seemed as if a tornado invaded your life emotionally, and some of your assurances seem distant. Jesus understands. He was tempted in all ways, just like we are, and He overcame. Let's learn from His example.

According to the Gospel of Matthew, immediately after Jesus was baptized, there were two specific events: the Spirit descended on Jesus like a dove, and an audible voice was heard by Him and others who stood nearby. The voice was that of His Father, announcing to the world that this was His Son, and He was very pleased with Him. Father solidified and affirmed Jesus' identity, not only to Jesus but to all who were listening. Jesus also received the empowerment of the Holy Spirit in the same event. Abruptly, that same lovely gentle Dove, Holy Spirit, proceeds to lead Him into a wild place to be tested by His enemy.

That doesn't seem fair.

In Matthew 4:3-10, the enemy attacks the very word Father God spoke over Jesus: *if you are the Son of God*....he says this three times. The enemy addressed physical needs, challenged His unconditional love and trust in the Father, and desired Jesus to short circuit His destiny. The enemy was pushing Him to step out of relationship with the Father and to take His life into His own hands.

"If you are this, then just do this for Your own sake." The enemy's strategy is an insidious ploy, taking the truth and sliding it toward self-reliance rather than continuing to get insight from heaven.

In verse 4, we see something pretty amazing. Jesus was basically saying: I don't just live so My body can be comfortable, but I do live by every word that comes from the mouth of Dad. That word here is the Greek word *rhema*, "that which is spoken." It is the now word of the Lord that He speaks for your situation at a certain point of time (Ephesians 6:17). Jesus' bottom line was: "I don't hear Dad saying I'm supposed to be making bread." Father knows that Jesus is hungry; it's just that the provision for Jesus' strengthening had not completely played out yet. It implies that in a relationship with God, you are continually hearing.

If the enemy is attacking your identity and attempting to steal from you (which is his constant modus operandi), what is your *rhema* word? Ask the Lord to give you key Scriptures with which you fight with and stand on in faith. Usually, these *rhema* words come as a quick thought in your mind. They might come as you are reading the Bible, and Scriptures leap off the page and bring life. Decree and declare them with your mouth. The more you proclaim them, the deeper your faith matures, and satan backs off.

In Luke 4:14, we read an interesting ending to the temptations. Jesus returned in the power of the Spirit. As you war with your *rhema* word, there is the promise of power in the Holy Spirit as an exchange. Each time you fight for your identity using your *rhema* word, you become stronger.

When you have been attacked with confusion concerning your destiny or identity, go to prayer and ask God for your "now" (*rhema*) word with which to fight off the enemy's attacks. Write those Scriptures here.

If you have had an inner healing session, go back to the words God gave you concerning your freedom. Declare them out loud and pray them back to God. "Lord, You said _____ and I receive this and know that this truth will become stronger in my spirit daily. I know that You will give me *rhema* words if the enemy tempts me. Thank You for my breakthrough. As I press in close to You, I know You will continue to affirm my identity."

Prayer:

Thank You Lord that You are making me aware when the enemy wants to rob me. I will guard my house with a knowledge of Your protective presence and the words You have spoken over me. You are a strong tower of protection for me.

Day 2: **Sideswiped**

The day is going along great, and suddenly you get sideswiped! Where did that come from? Perhaps it's a feeling of unrest, anxious thoughts, or even crippling fear. Ever want to run away? Escape? Take a nap? Have confusing thoughts flooded over you, making you dizzy? I have. But I'm getting better at recognizing the source of some of these sucker punches.

"...When the enemy comes in like a flood, the Spirit of the Lord will lift up a standard against him" (Isaiah 59:19). What is that standard? The truth. Ask the Lord, "What lie am I believing about You or me?"

Several years ago, I developed a crippling fear of going over highway overpasses. Actually, I always had a steely grip on the steering wheel whenever I had to drive over them, but somehow seemed to gut it through. After a particularly traumatic experience, I could no longer tough it out and would find the craziest back roads to avoid overpasses, especially in large cities. I confided this to a friend and asked her to accompany me to Dallas so she could pray while I drove. We got caught on one overpass going incredibly slow, and she started to laugh. Not me. I was shaking, crying, and thought I was going to pass out.

For the next several years, I avoided overpasses like the plague. Finally, determined to try and conquer my fear again, I decided to take a large, long overpass on my way home. *Oh my! God, I need help!* In my best authoritative voice, I shouted at the top of my lungs, "Fear, I rebuke you in the name of Jesus." I made it without passing out, but I was dissatisfied. The fear remained. I asked the Lord for a specific key.

Here is what I heard: "Greater are You, Jesus, in me than the fear that is trying to attack me." I recalled the Scripture in 1 John 4:4, *". .He who is in you is greater than he who is in the world."*

Did you notice the shift in perspective? I no longer looked at the fear, but at Jesus. I didn't fight fear, I looked at Peace! You should know that I drive overpasses quite calmly now. Does the enemy still try to attack me? Yes, but I look at Jesus. I declare out loud that He loves me, desires to protect me, gives me strength, knows my weakness, and can make me strong. I had believed the lie that He wasn't big enough to help me. When I looked at Him, the fear became smaller and finally dissipated. I made a choice. I turned away from the problem and focused on all that He has given me.

Are there any places in your heart, mind, or spirit where you are fixated on the problem rather than the solution (Him)? Ask Him. He is faithful to answer. Write your responses in the space provided.

- Ask the Lord what lie you might be believing.

- List previous solutions you've tried.

- Take one fixated problem, and write a new solution to try.

- Ask Jesus what He wants to say about this situation.

- Write down any verses the Lord may give on 3x5 cards to carry with you.

- Loudly proclaim your verses whenever the problem tries to arise.

Prayer:

Lord, when fear or a lie comes to steal my peace, help me to turn my back to it and look at You. The answers always lie in You and Your amazing insight, compassion, and tender love. Thank You, Lord, for Your constant encouragement to look only to You for my solutions.

Day 3: **Eyes Fixed on Jesus**

". . .Since we are surrounded by so great a cloud of witnesses, [powerful men and women of faith who have gone before us], *let us lay aside every weight, and the sin which so easily ensnares us, and let us run with endurance the race that is set before us, looking unto Jesus, the author and finisher of our faith. . ."* (Hebrews 12:1-2a, brackets mine).

> *"Trust in the Lord with all your heart, and lean not on your own understanding; in all your ways, acknowledge Him and He shall direct your paths" (Proverbs 3:5-6).*

When I first learned to drive, the instructor explained that my driving would be smoother if I looked ahead about five car lengths down the road. I would sense everything around me and have time to make corrections if necessary. He was right. When I kept my eyes out front, peripheral vision picked up everything else.

I believe it's the same principle with Jesus. If we keep looking at Him, acknowledging Him in each situation, checking in with Him, asking Holy Spirit for counsel and direction while driving through life, we find our paths become straighter. We avoid obstacles that cause harm. There is less chance of fear and panic latching on that could roll us off our paths. Our Father is always calling us forward to new realms of intimacy and adventures with Him.

Psalm 32:8 says: *"I will instruct you and teach you in the way you should go; I will guide you with My eye."* People who have known each other a long time and have developed a strong sense of trust, can often times know what the other is thinking by just glancing at their eyes. This intimacy can translate into knowing how a person feels in any situation. This is the level of friendship and trust Father, Jesus, and Holy Spirit want with you. What a wonderful place of vulnerability and trust with our Savior.

Keep looking to the author and finisher of your faith. Forget those things which are behind and press forward to the high calling He has for you, keeping your eyes on Him (my paraphrase of Hebrews 12:2a, Philippians 3:13-14).

Questions to ponder.

- What does it mean to keep my eyes on Jesus?

- List up to three times you have been successful keeping your eyes on Jesus during difficult times.

- What did I learn from that?

Prayer

Father, help me to lean in and look at You when I feel unsure. I want to look deep into Your eyes and see Your desire for me. I embrace Your affection and love for me. I will continue to look for Your ways and Your kingdom.

Day 4: **We Become What We Behold**

After years of staying away from video games, I found one on my new phone. Do I dare? I tentatively opened the app and thoroughly enjoyed my first game. I enjoyed another and another, daily. The thrill of completing each level offset some stress, and I believed the game was the perfect down-time distraction. Being a smidge competitive, it became more and more difficult to stop. What shocked me most was when I would close my eyes to concentrate or go to sleep, I would envision the maze and strategize the next move. My brain, thoughts, and imagination reflected what I was spending time on. This shocked and concerned me. The game itself was teaching me a spiritual truth.

> *"And we all, with unveiled face, continually seeing as in a mirror the glory of the Lord, are progressively being transformed into His image from [one degree of] glory to [even more] glory, which comes from the Lord, [who is] the Spirit"*
>
> *(2 Corinthians 3:18, AMP).*

We become what we behold. Our minds eventually reflect what we look at or meditate on. As we gaze at His glory, we are changed to look like Him. Ever notice how married couples who have been together a long time begin to have the same mannerisms, voice inflections, or verbal responses to situations? Same with the Lover of our souls. The more we hang out with Him in worship, praying in the Spirit, reading His written Word, we are reflecting His thoughts, ways, and responses.

When we keep our eyes on His eyes, lean into His presence, allow ourselves to be vulnerable to His voice, we begin to notice what else He is looking at and our eyes will follow His eyes. His voice always encourages and invites us in closer.

Question to ask. Write your answer below.

Is what I am gazing at and concentrating on changing me into His likeness?

Prayer

Lord, I am responding to Your invitation to come closer and closer, to feel Your breath and know Your heart. I want to see what You are looking at and place my gaze there so that I look and become more like You. I love You so much Lord. Thank You that You, the Creator of the universe, want to hang out with me!

Day 5: **Sound of Truth**

How much do you pay attention to the sounds around you? Do you tune into the birds singing, traffic noises, or bacon sizzling? What do you hear when you speak? The power of sound is evident at creation. God spoke, and creation began. What was not seen became visible; calling those things that were not as though they were. Even quantum physics experiments prove that sound affects solid matter at the smallest molecular level. Why is this important to know? You were created in His image and so have the same creative power with your words.

Our words continue to reverberate into the spiritual atmosphere long after they are spoken and have the power to affect our future. How do I know this? In Mark 4:24, Jesus instructs us to be careful what we hear. He also says that whatever we say, when we believe, we shall have (Matt 21:22). And if that's not enough, in Proverbs 18:21, we learn the power of the tongue to bring life or death.

Recently, I walked through an extremely tough year in my life. I was still recovering from major surgery. My job was very demanding. And on top of that, my husband went through two major surgeries which required long, difficult recovery periods. I was unraveling emotionally because of no sleep and the constant pulls on me from every direction. I began whining out loud, and it scared me. Have you ever whined out loud? I invested in two books by Steve and Wendy Backlund: *Victorious Mindsets* and *Igniting Faith in 40 Days*. I resolved to rise 30 minutes earlier each morning before work to read the devotionals and declare who I was in Jesus. Daily I verbally spoke and prayed the biblical decrees listed in the books over myself, my family, and my work situation.

The first few days I was inspired without measure! The next few weeks I was tired without measure! But I kept plodding on because I knew speaking truth over my spirit was giving me life whether or not I felt it manifested. Eventually, change snuck up on me! My joy in Him and His joy in me became my strength! Peace and calm invaded my circumstances. My thoughts were now grounded in His victory through me. I began to believe and act upon the truth about me from His perspective, not what my emotions and circumstances were trying to dictate. The atmospheres around me no longer controlled me.

Receive God's truth about who you are and declare it with your voice to yourself and to the atmosphere! You are creating platforms for God to spring you forward in increased freedom and joy.

Ask yourself:

What words have I spoken lately?

Are they bringing life?

Prayer

Lord, I am so thankful that You are making me aware of my words and what I say. I repent for all the times I have said negative words over my life. I forgive those who didn't speak positively into my life. I make a choice to speak life over every area of my being and arena of influence. You are the author of life, and I desire to partner with You throughout my life.

Day 6: **Hoping in God's Goodness**

Hope is defined as a confident expectation of good. Are you at the place where you can definitely say...*God is good, all the time*?

A friend was working through this and making good progress. She turned off the voice that wanted to drain her faith and began to *confidently*, *expectantly* look for examples of God's goodness.

My friend planned a trip outside the country with a verbal commitment that her visa for entry was coming. She purchased the airfare, and her timetable was winding down to departure. Still no visa. The evening before her scheduled departure, she came to my home to pick up an item I wanted to send with her for a church in the area. She had expertly packed, things were in storage, and she was confident she would receive the needed visa before her afternoon departure. She was radiant with expectation!

"Christy, I have no stress or worry, it's amazing." We prayed, hugged, and I sent her on her way. We connected the next morning and still no visa. I could hear the sigh in her voice as she listed all the hoops she would have to jump through to re-schedule her flight as well as the higher cost and inconvenience. She admitted hearing a voice that said, "Well, God could have made that visa show up if He had really wanted to."

Stirring up her faith, she resisted the whisper of doubt and declared aloud, "God, I know You can make that visa appear! But even if the visa doesn't arrive, I trust You to work all this out for good. I choose to trust You." She returned to her office where the question of the visa came up. Her co-worker mentioned that she had seen an envelope with my friend's name on it. The visa was inside, hidden from view in a cupboard!

What is the point of this story? She trusted God's goodness, however He chose to work it through. She declared His goodness with her mouth and chose to stay in worship. This attracts God's presence which always results in hope! Think she has a book of remembrance of His goodness now? You bet.

Hope. Confidently looking – not a casual glance— rather, searching with an intention of finding good. In your inner healing session, God said wonderful things to you. Actively proclaim with your voice to the spiritual world what He declared over you. Be proactive. Anticipate the expression of His goodness in your life and circumstances. The goal of His voice is to set you free.

Some action steps:

- Spend several minutes declaring the goodness of God with a thankful spirit, remembering times when you experienced His goodness displayed.
- Express your gratefulness for what He has spoken over you and will speak in the future.
- Sing your favorite worship song to the Lord.
- Declare that you will see the goodness of the Lord in the land of the living. Confidently expect to see His goodness!

Prayer

Thank You, Lord, that You are always speaking because You are continuously interceding for me and desiring me to see You in all Your goodness.

Day 7: **Two Powerful Weapons**

I struggled to see how God was going to rescue us from this financial predicament. We were living by faith, all of the bills were paid, but there were no promises of any future income any time soon. Lord, the savings will be gone eventually! What are we going to do? I stilled my heart and waited for an answer. It came immediately in the form of a memory.

We had sold most of our personal belongings and were packing up to join Youth With A Mission (YWAM). Our pastor wasn't too thrilled, though. We were over $300,000 in debt! We knew we had a word from the Lord, so continued to move forward and do all we could to straighten out the finances. Within three weeks, we sold three buildings, paid some bills and had other bills wiped clean. Needless to say, we had our pastor's blessing at our departure. That memory inspired faith into my present circumstances, along with hope and joy.

One of our powerful weapons is hope. It is the confident expectation that God is bringing good. How do we acquire hope? We can go through our personal book of remembrance—previous testimonies when God has sovereignly intervened and brought about a deliverance. If you haven't started documenting your testimonies, do so now. This can be written in a journal or recorded on a device.

Revelation 19:10b says, *"Worship God! For the testimony of Jesus is the spirit of prophecy."* He did it once, He can do it again. This is the way David strengthened himself in the Lord. All through the Psalms, when feeling defeated and abused, David remembered all the times God had intervened in his life: *"Bless the Lord, O my soul; and all that is within me, bless His holy name...And forget not all His benefits"* (Psalm 103: 1,2b). Coupled with worship and praise, he declared with his voice the testimony back to the Lord.

Then David would do the bold faith-filled act. He confidently and expectantly looked for the answer. We too can be proactive this way; it is called faith in the goodness of God. If you are still questioning the goodness of the Lord, ask Him what lie you are believing and break agreement with it. When He shows you the truth, be sure to write it down in your book of remembrance. Ask Him for specific Scriptures that will be exact keys for you.

A second powerful weapon is joy. Think about this: God takes enjoyment in me, my personhood, my uniqueness, my quirks, my likes, and dislikes...*this* is what gives me strength! *". . . The joy of the Lord is your strength"* (Nehemiah 8:10b). When I am completely and unconditionally loved, it infuses me with courage and anticipation. I confidently listen for His voice because He is always for me, not against me. Because He is for me, the next moment is full of unique possibilities, new thought processes, and new paradigms. Creative avenues are presented from His heart. Again, I am proactively looking, proclaiming, and declaring my thought processes to line up with heaven's perspective.

We choose to renew our minds daily. We choose to line up with truth and not fall back into old ruts and trenches that have kept us bound. We are not at the mercy of anything. Romans 8:37 declares, *". . .We are more than conquerors through Him who loved us."*

Ask yourself: How am I being strengthened by God's joy in me?

Prayer

Thank You, Lord, that hope and joy are amazing swords for fighting off lies and fears. When the enemy comes to accuse me or malign Your character, help me to remember my past victories and to impart faith to me that You will do it again. Thank You that You are abundantly available for help in tight places.

Day 8: **Overcoming Temptation**

No temptation [regardless of its source] *has overtaken or enticed you that is not common to human experience* [nor is any temptation unusual or beyond human resistance]; *but God is faithful* [to His Word—He is compassionate and trustworthy], *and He will not let you be tempted beyond your ability* [to resist], *but along with the temptation He* [has in the past and is now and] *will* [always] *provide the way out as well, so that you will be able to endure it* [without yielding, and will overcome temptation with joy] *Therefore, my beloved, run* [keep far, far away] *from* [any sort of] *idolatry* [and that includes loving anything more than God, or participating in anything that leads to sin and enslaves the soul]. (1 Corinthians 10:13-14, AMP).

Highlight key words in this passage that stood out to you. Now rewrite this verse in your own words.

We are promised that we will never be tested, tried, or attacked beyond our ability and strength to resist. Notice the *therefore* in this passage. Was it one of the words you highlighted? A great teacher once said: anytime you see the word, *therefore*, find out what it is there for!

Our kind, gracious, compassionate, and wise Father knows our strength and knows what we can handle. He has promised He will never lead us into a fight we can't win. He is also waiting to see if we can say no to that which desires to control us.

Is there an emotion, mindset, thought pattern, memory, or person that is guarding your devotion more than your relationship to your loving heavenly Father, your precious elder brother Jesus, or your compassionate counselor and teacher, Holy Spirit? Like a puppet on a string, can you be pulled and pushed emotionally by any idolatry? Sometimes we forge an identity about ourselves around a past event, person, or mindset. God desires our identity to be found in Him alone. Anything else is idolatry.

And what are our instructions for avoiding idolatry? Turn away, reject, spurn, cut the strings! God says He gave you that ability and strength and knows you will find the way to escape the entrapment. Jesus died to give you your identity by looking at Him. Once you see who He is, you will know who you are!

Some action steps:

- Inquire of the Lord if there is anything that "pushes your buttons." Wait patiently to see if He brings anything to mind. Write it here.

- Ask Him how it got there and why it still influences you.

- Repent, forgive if necessary, and break agreement with it. Ask God to show you the truth.

- If He doesn't reveal anything, rejoice that you have His promise that you have a place to land when you flee the temptation!

- Where is that safe place for you?

Prayer

Lord, I declare through Your blood, I can break any stronghold latching onto my life. Like Philippians 4:13, I proclaim: "I can do all things through Christ who strengthens me." I assert Your truth is always there for me and ever will be. I pronounce that Holy Spirit resides in me and gives me wisdom when I need it. Thank You that You are my rock and anchor.

Day 9: **Destination Disease**

Have you ever said something similar to this?

- "When I can finally get over this, then I'll be free and happy."
- "When I lose those last 10 pounds, I will feel successful."
- "When I get married, I will finally feel fulfilled and truly loved."

One of my favorite authors, Steve Backlund, calls this Destination Disease. The chief complaint? "I can't be happy until_____" (Fill in the blank.)

In some dysfunctional way, many of us view this as goal setting. I know I did. I thought this way from my teenage years through most of my adult life. I saw my struggles, hard places, difficult relationships, and personal failures as times when I just needed to push through. I expected I would find fulfillment on the other side. I had no idea how self-centered and self-reliant this thinking was nor how much joy I missed in the journey.

Peace, joy, and contentment aren't necessarily found in your circumstances or your environment although we can have portions of these desires fulfilled as situations unfold. What I came to realize was my joy wouldn't be found at the destination but in the person of Jesus. I needed to partner with Him in my journey. By looking to the desired outcome for strength rather than walking with Him who is *all strength*, I was forfeiting my serenity and His perspective.

Peace comes from the Prince of Peace. Joy comes from the One who sings over me. Contentment comes from walking with Him who cares for me more than the birds of the air. *"Are you not of more value than they?"* (Matthew 6:26b).

Fulfillment—peace, contentment, joy—comes from *not* looking at what isn't resolved, but from looking at and walking with the lover of my soul. He desires that I prosper and be in health, even as my soul prospers (3 John 1:2). He who began a good work in you will be faithful to complete it (Philippians 1:6).

Questions to ponder:

Are you infected with Destination Disease?

If you are infected, what is it that you say?

Ask the Lord, how do you want me to give this to You?

Prayer

Lord, I thank You that I don't have to be infected with Destination Disease. I declare there is joy in the journey because You are holding my hand. There is nothing too difficult for You. Show me where You are today in my journey.

Day 10: **Praying our Desires**

Hope deferred makes the heart sick, but a longing fulfilled is a tree of life (Proverbs 13:12, NIV).

May he give you the desire of your heart and make all your plans succeed (Psalm 20:4, NIV).

He fulfills the desires of those who fear him; he hears their cry and saves them (Psalm 145:19, NIV).

In one sentence, write below what you think God is saying through these three Scriptures.

In the previous section on Destination Disease, we spoke of joy in the journey by walking and talking with Him who knows us best. We decided not to lose our joy by succumbing to a Destination Disease, but would instead retain our joy by staying in the eternal *now* with Him, hearing His heartbeat, voice, and perspective. By meditating on the verses above, we can see that our desires are vital to Him. So how do we pursue Him about our longings?

First, let's look at a Destination Disease:
"When my housing arrangement changes, then I can finally relax and be happy."

Second, what do we find by digging deeper into this statement? Perhaps privacy issues, social acceptance or interference, financial issues, or space to grow.

Third, digging even deeper, we might find desires for security, belonging, feeling heard, being valued. This third level of revelation is where our authentic yearnings lie. God longs to hear these requests and intentionally wants to fulfill them.

Back to the question: How do we pursue Him about our desires? We have to be willing to go to the root of the longing, and ask ourselves: *Why* do I desire this? What is it I really want and need to have fulfilled? We ask questions based on getting to know our Savior better in relationship. We are designed by Him to have our longings fulfilled in relationship to Him, not in a situation. I learned this from another author I admire, Tony Stoltzfus when I read his book, *Questions for Jesus: Conversational Prayer Around Your Deepest Desires.*

Ask yourself: What am I longing for? Is it peace?

If so, then ask: "Lord, where are you in this situation? How do I find you, Prince of Peace? May I have some of your peace?"

Is it belonging?

Ask: "Lord, will You show me how You feel about me?"

Is it being heard?

Ask: "Lord, how do You feel when I pray?"

Is it feeling significant?

Ask: "Lord, how did You feel when You designed me?"

When you hear from Papa God, your true heart's desires are being addressed. It is from this place that you are empowered to find His joy in the journey.

Prayer

Lord, would You help me to find my true desires? Help me formulate the questions that You know would thrill my heart with Your answers. Lord, I will write down what You say and read it often to encourage myself.

Day 11: **Acquitted of Guilt**

Therefore, since we have been justified [that is, acquitted of sin, declared blameless before God] *by faith,* [let us grasp the fact that] *we have peace with God* [and the joy of reconciliation with Him] *through our Lord Jesus Christ* [the Messiah, the Anointed] (Romans 5:1, AMP).

As you meditate on this, rewrite it in your own words. Make a declaration about yourself. Take by faith, bold faith, that you are justified, seen just as if you've never sinned. There is no guilt or shame over you. When your spirit fully perceives this, you open a door to receive the encouragement and freedom of God. The wall has been broken down, and He is making you into a bold warrior who knows how to do everything in His strength.

Romans 5:1-5 says I access my justification, peace, and grace by faith. This passage also speaks of rejoicing in "pressings" which have a way of developing something that perhaps no other circumstance can...proving my character and producing hope. Hope can only come when I refuse the lie that God isn't good.

Meditate on this verse:

> *". . .All things work together for good to those who love God, to those who are the called according to His purposes (Romans 8:28).*

Ask the Lord:

In what ways would You like to encourage me and take me higher?

What has been lost for me, Lord, that I can trust You to turn around for good?

Prayer

It is amazing Lord that my identity is not linked to guilt or shame, but to freedom. Show me more and more ways that I can believe and walk out this truth.

Day 12: Combination Thinking

I had a rough time recovering from an intense situation, and I prayed out loud about it. I took authority over thoughts of condemnation that I knew came from the enemy. But every time I tried to say the word condemnation, it came out *combination*. It suddenly dawned on me that the Lord was trying to tell me something.

Combination thinking is allowing thoughts of two opposing forces to wage war in my mind. Knowing the truth was one thing. Allowing another thought to come up alongside it to beat me up was quite another. These thoughts begin with:
"Yeah, but you..."
"You should have..."
"Why didn't you..."

Voices that accuse, belittle, shame, and bring with them a stench of hopelessness are *always* from the enemy's camp. I knew the perspective of truth in my situation but allowed the whispers of the enemy to come in and try to "combine" with the truth. These other ideas twisted my rationale, creating confusion and frustration. That is what combining truth and lies does: it robs, kills, and destroys vision. And, it stops forward movement into God's perspective and solutions.

Repent *(mentally change directions 180°)* for allowing any combination thinking to invade your mind. Ask the Lord to give you His grace to discern it immediately. There really is no competition to the truth unless you allow it in. Take a firm stand and say a strong yes to truth. Speak His truth about you and your situation. Immerse yourself in His Word. War with the prophetic words over your life. Declare truth with your voice.

Some action steps:

- Can you think of a time when you allowed combination thinking?

- What was the outcome of that thinking: Did it bring life or confusion?

- What can you do in the future that will keep you from combination thinking?

Prayer

Lord, thank You! Thank You for redeeming me from lies and ushering me into the truth of how You feel about me. Thank You for Your Word that continually instructs me how You think, therefore illuminating how I need to think. I am renewing my mind with Your thoughts. Thank You, Daddy God, that light is stronger than darkness any day, and that I am more than a conqueror because of Your death and resurrection. I cast away from me all combination thinking. I choose You and Your Truth.

Day 13: **Panic Produces Blindness**

Not long ago, I worked in the shoe department of a popular department store. I had to work the stock room for three weeks before I was allowed to sell any shoes. This was to familiarize me with the location of shoes that had only one on display to the public. Theoretically, this was to enable me to easily find the shoes any given customer should want to try on in her size. I say theoretically because what the customer didn't know was that there were acres of shoes out of sight on the other side of the wall. They were categorized by color and then heel height. The largest category was the black shoes—their shelves seem to go on forever—and every time I stepped into the vast sea of black, I felt swallowed up, claustrophobic, and confined.

Knowing there was a customer waiting anxiously for wonderful news of their desired shoe, I felt pressured to hurry, search quickly, deliver good or bad news, and perhaps find another shoe similar so as not to lose the sale. However, I found myself panicking when my hunt didn't produce the shoe rapidly. I would scan the walls again and again but to no avail. I would finally humble myself and ask for help from one of my co-workers who usually would walk right up to it and hand it to me. How humiliated I was on numerous occasions. Why can't I see what I'm looking for? One day, I walked to the black abyss and whispered a prayer: "God, help me to see what I'm looking for; I choose not to panic but trust You. Help me slow down and reject fear and pressure." Guess what? I found the shoe. That's when I realized that panic produces blindness.

Have you ever had an experience where you felt fearful, oppressed, even like you were suffocating? Write your answer here.

When given free reign, fear can turn to panic and become an overpowering force.

Fear of failure, fear of ignorance, fear of timing.

Panic cripples and produces nothing of value.

Fear overshadows and obscures thinking until you are unable to perceive truth.

Fear entertained eventually brings blindness. It will cause us to act hastily, not out of wisdom. Many times, fear will push us into our own thought processes and not those of God.

Timothy says fear is a spirit. *For God has not given us a spirit of fear, but of power and of love and of a sound mind* (2 Timothy 1:7). You have authority over fear. Resist it, cast it out, and it will flee from you. Draw near to the One who loves you the most, and He will fill the void with Himself.

> **"I am the [only] Way [to God] and the [real] Truth and the [real] Life; no one comes to the Father but through Me (John 14:6, AMP).**

Take a deep breath, boldly take hold of the truth He has revealed to you, and continue to walk in your freedom. If any panic tries to knock at your door, don't answer!

- Is there a thought process that you entertain that wants to produce panic?

- In what situation can you take a deep breath and choose faith over fear?

- Recount a time you were rescued and felt safe.

- Draw a picture of the place of peace where you felt safe.

Prayer

Lord, help me to snuggle up in Your Spirit to that place of peace where You connected with me. Help me to remember what You have given me to replace fear. I cast all my cares on You because I know You care for me.

Day 14: **The Great Redeemer**

In Genesis 18:12-15, we find an interesting scenario. Sarah is eavesdropping on a conversation between her husband and the Lord. God tells Abraham that Sarah is going to have a son next year. Sarah starts laughing. . .doesn't He know she is 90 years old? The Lord confronts her laughter, and she denies it. Fast forward to Hebrews 11:11 where Sarah is remembered as a woman of faith *". . . Because she judged Him faithful who had promised."*

Whoa! Did God miss something here? King David commits adultery and murder and later is described by God as a man after His own heart. *"For a righteous man falls seven times, and rises again. . ."* (Proverbs 24:16a, AMP). God never berates you in your failures. In His book of remembrance, you are celebrated as the person who pressed through with Him.

Nothing is ever lost in the kingdom because God is our Great Redeemer. He knows how to buy back what we believe to be lost forever—either due to our poor choices or the enemy's thieving. What He restores may not look the same; often it is better. *". . . All things work together for good. . ."* (Romans 8:28).

Believe by bold faith that you are seen just as if you've never sinned. When understood, this opens a door to receive the encouragement of God. He is making you into a courageous warrior who knows how to stand, and then gives you the *ability* to stand your ground. The Word of God says, *". . .there is now no condemnation for those who are in Christ Jesus. . ."* (Romans 8:1, NIV).

Prayer

Lord, how do You see me? Show me any area of unbelief or failure where I am condemning myself.

Declare this aloud:

Precious Father, I renounce agreement with any lies that You are a withholder, stingy, or a punisher. I refuse to listen to falsehoods that tell me You are a harsh enforcer. I break, shatter, and destroy any thoughts that say I must be perfect or You won't show up, rescue, teach, inform, or be present. Teach me to walk in vulnerable humility, allowing You to touch any area of my life that isn't pleasing to You. I yearn for intimacy with You as my great reward.

Day 15: **Higher Perspective**

> *"If then you were raised with Christ,*
> *seek those things which are above,*
> *where Christ is, sitting at the right*
> *hand of God" (Colossians 3:1).*

"[God] raised us up together, and made us sit together in the heavenly places in Christ Jesus" (Ephesians 2:6).

According to the Scriptures above, where are you seated? Ask Jesus to give you a picture of what that looks like.

There is something about looking at a place from a high position that gives perspective. We are instructed to not just look at our present circumstances, but to look from Heaven's angle. What is God's point of view? We are above, not beneath; we are the head, not the tail. As Romans 8:37 declares: *". . .we are more than conquerors through Him who loved us."* <u>These are not just words.</u> God spoke, and there was life!

When God speaks, we can trust those words to be solid substance! Take hold of the words He has spoken over you. Speak them again and again over yourself. You will soon begin to observe change in your perspective. This higher viewpoint will change your life.

Some action points:

List a time in your life when God spoke, and profound things happened.

Is there an area in your life where you need a higher perspective?

Prayer

Lord, help me to gain Your perspective in areas where I may be too close to see and perceive correctly. I step up to sit in Your lap. I desire to see from Your viewpoint all the areas of victory You have for me.

Day 16: **Roar Back!**

"God is not a man that He should lie. . ." (Numbers 23:19). God most always takes the initiative to speak into your life, thereby confirming His love, awareness, and solutions for you.

> **"Believe in the Lord your God, and you shall be established; believe His prophets, and you shall prosper"** **(2 Chronicles 20:20b).**

The enemy prowls around roaring. His only agenda is to steal your peace and rob you of your joy. Take your words and roar back! Pace the floor and yell if you have to. I've done this many times.

If you saw the popular, blockbuster movie WAR ROOM in the summer of 2015, you heard Priscilla Shirer "roar at the devil." In the film, she is fighting for her marriage and learning that prayer is a powerful weapon. In one dramatic scene, she storms outside, yelling at the enemy:

"I don't know where you are, devil. You have played with my man... No more! You are done. Jesus is the Lord of this house, and that means there's no place for you here anymore. So take your lies... your accusations and get out in Jesus' name... My joy is found in Jesus, and just in case you forgot, He has already defeated you, so go back to hell where you belong and leave my family alone!" (Source: Internet Movie Database - imdb)

Go on the offensive with no intimidation. Your emotions will catch up with what your spirit is declaring.

Roar back, dear saint! Hold your ground! Ask the Lord to show you where you need to stand firm and what words you need to roar.

Pray out loud

Thank You, Lord, that every time the enemy tries to intimidate me with a loud roar, You have enabled me to choose life and roar back.

Based on this, write your own prayer that will help you to roar.

Day 17: **He Knows My Name**

> *"Call to Me, and I will answer you, and show you great and mighty things, which you do not know" (Jeremiah 33:3).*

I heard this Scripture in my mind as I headed to my room. My husband took the kids to lunch while I waited to see what God wanted to say to me. The word *call* in this instance means to cry out, to address someone; to shout or speak out. It often describes calling out loudly in an attempt to get someone's attention or calling on the Lord or upon His name.

I thought, "Okay, I'll just call out His name." Softly and tentatively at first, I said, "Jesus." As I continued saying His name, I allowed my voice to get slightly louder and more determined. As I paused, I heard an amazing thing. To this day, I don't know if it was in my mind or actually audible, but I heard Him say my name! He said it twice. And oh, the way He said it! The tone and inflection carried the most intense affection and caring.

When He said my name, it was like I was an open book and He knew every single detail of my life and still loved me! I felt precious in His sight. Waves and waves of His love washed over me. He knows me and still likes me. Barbs of rejection were being pulled out by this intimate knowledge of how He feels about me. I wept and wept. It was the beginning of Him showing me great and mighty things, emotions I couldn't see or perceive or even pinpoint. It is a journey I continue to pursue today. Oh, to know Him more!

I love because I know I am so completely and utterly, without reservation, loved by Him. Following this encounter, Father God continued to take me places where pain or loss had affected me and brought His presence to that incident to give me a new memory.

Allow God to take you on a journey to show you splendid and hidden things so He can show Himself strong on your behalf. When we call, He answers. He knows your name.

• What would I like to explore with God? Write your response below.

- What hidden things would You like to show me today Lord?

Prayer

Thank You, Lord, that according to Psalm 139, You know me inside and out. You know my every thought, and I am never invisible to You. Your love carries me, and You uphold me with Your hand. Lord, I am asking that this knowledge go past head information to heart transformation.

Day 18: **Dreams and Visions**

Memories can be good, bad, or indifferent. They can also be lost or suppressed. Many times in inner healing, memories surface that have been long forgotten. Some of the suppression comes to protect ourselves. Some just because we didn't feel it was important enough to store in a brain file to be retrieved later. What is amazing, though, is that God can create new memories and supersede previous memories. He is not restricted by time.

I had an amazing father. He enjoyed engaging with people and enjoyed a good laugh. He was generous with his physical resources. He found pleasure working his retail stores and had an amazing marketing mind. There was one area, though, that was difficult for him. As a daughter, I longed to sit in his lap and be hugged, call him Daddy and told that I was beautiful and special. For whatever reason, this was something he could not give. So I grew up with an empty spot in my heart that I didn't know how to fill.

But my Heavenly Father knew my need. I began to get brave in my quiet times with Him and prayed like this: "Daddy God, can You give me what I need in this area of my heart? I forgive and release my earthly father for what he could not give. What would You like to give me in return?"

My Heavenly Father would take me on wonderful journeys with Him. Call it visions or an actual physical trip. I have been swimming with Him, picnics on grass, strolling through fields of multi-colored flowers (my favorite), or just burying my face in His neck while sitting on His lap. In every instance, He looks me straight in the eyes and tells me something He likes about me. I am connected with Him emotionally and feel safe, secure, loved, and valuable. Sometimes I am an adult, other times a child. Every time I "go" with Him, that place in my heart that used to be empty gets filled with new memories.

My new memories are giving me a firm foundation for a healthy identity and a more intimate walk with the Godhead. This isn't unique to me. In 2 Corinthians 12, Paul said he went to heaven and saw incredible things. This can be yours as well. You are already seated with Him in heavenly places. You can go beyond the torn veil to the place you are seated with Him. You can also know and experience the Lover of your soul. He is ready to meet your every need.

Some action points:

What place in your heart would you like the Godhead to fill with new memories?

Ask God, "Can I 'go' places with you too?"

Prayer

Lord, thank You that You came to fill all those places in my heart that long for more. I thank You that You want me to know You in a deeper way than I did yesterday. Whether in night dreams or pictures during the day, let us enjoy amazing adventures together. I thank You in advance that You know how to love me well and love me into wellness.

Day 19: **Power Boost**

I am so grateful for my prayer language. When I asked Holy Spirit to baptize me with Himself, there was no super amazing emotions or reactions. My new prayer language consisted of two words. Really God? How was I going to pray with two words? I assumed "it didn't take," and basically just put the whole tongues thing on the shelf. I did obtain an insatiable thirst for the Word. It seemed like I was reading the Bible for the first time with a Friend who guided me through every verse.

About two years later, after reading and re-reading Acts and Corinthians, I realized I might be missing out by not praying in the Spirit in tongues. So I began sheepishly praying my two words over and over. After several weeks, as I attached faith to my words, my vocabulary increased. As I have pressed into God, especially in times of need, while praying in tongues, I would receive insight and answers to my secret, unspoken prayers. Revelation into situations and His wisdom seemed to flow into my spirit so effortlessly. There were even times I asked God if I could interpret my tongues, and I was dumbfounded at what I heard. I was praying beautiful expressions of praise, adoration, and worship.

Wow, my spirit really knew how to communicate with my amazing Savior. I now make it a point to pray in the Spirit often. In the shower, on my walks with the dog, before I go to sleep at night. I would suggest that your spirit knows exactly how to communicate with Him too. The hidden treasures of His kingdom are yours, and He delights to give them to you. Take a moment to look up and read Jude 1:20 and 1 Corinthians 14:4. Did you receive any new insights about speaking in tongues?

A friend of mine recounted a story to me. He shared with some friends about his prayer language. The couple flatly refused to believe that this gift was for today. Several weeks later, my friend received a phone call from the husband. The man related that he was driving his car, praying fervently about a situation, and suddenly began to speak in a different language. This so shocked him that he immediately pulled over and phoned his wife. He explained what had just transpired, and she exclaimed that she spontaneously started speaking in tongues as well just a few minutes earlier.

Your prayer language is part of building up your spirit to stay connected with His heart and kingdom culture. I encourage you to practice your unique language with Him. If your language hasn't manifested yet, no worries. He knows your heart and knows how to give you gifts at just the right time.

Lord, I would like a closer relationship with Holy Spirit. What would you like to give or say to me today?

Prayer

Thank You Holy Spirit for all Your gifts. I am available and willing to receive all that You desire to give and relax in Your wisdom and timing. I am holding out my hands like a small child to receive all of Your goodness. Walking with You is the most amazing adventure I could ever dream of. Thank You for always initiating love. Into Your hands, I commit my spirit.

Day 20: Liberty

When Adam and Eve disobeyed God in the garden, and He came to meet with them in the cool of the day, their first impulse was to hide behind leaves. I always found this interesting. Shame wants us to hide our true self. Whenever I want to hide, failure or inadequacy usually has been knocking on my door.

When Moses returned from spending time with God on Mount Sinai, his face shone with a unique radiance (Exodus 34:29-35). This frightened people, so he covered his face with a veil. Notice that he didn't feel a need to cover himself speaking face-to-face with God. He was totally free to be open and vulnerable before El Shaddai. He hid nothing from the Almighty of the Universe.

In 2 Corinthians 3:16-17, we read that whenever a person turns in repentance (changing your mind) to the Lord, the veil is stripped off and taken away. When face-to-face with the Spirit, there is freedom. What an amazing exchange! Changing our minds to agree with God's truth brings liberty. Shame and inadequacy have no place.

Just as the people were unnerved seeing the lingering presence and liberty on the face of Moses, don't be surprised if some people are noticing you and your newfound freedom walking with God. Those in prison usually have two opinions of those in freedom: resentment or a longing to obtain their freedom. Be ready to share with those who are hungry! Your freedom looks good on you!

Some action points

Have you ever wanted to hide in shame?

Are you aware that people are noticing your freedom?

Are you willing to share the joy and freedom you are experiencing?

Prayer

Lord, help me to discern those who are hungry for the freedom that I am now exhibiting. Help my light to stay on the hill and call to the ones who aren't sure they can be vulnerable. Keep me Holy Spirit in Your presence, so that the scent of my freedom draws others. Grant me the grace, wisdom, and boldness to share Your goodness today. I believe my freedom is for such a time as this.

Day 21: **Laughter**

"A happy heart is good medicine and a joyful mind causes healing. . ."

(Proverbs 17:22a, AMP).

On Sunday evenings, I would make it a point to turn on the TV and watch *America's Funniest Videos*. My husband would occasionally leave the room bored and work on something else. When he asked why I liked to watch such a silly show, my response surprised even me. I said, "I need to laugh out loud."

Behavioral scientists and medical professionals know the value of laughter and a cheerful heart. Bodies and minds heal faster when laughter is incorporated deliberately into life. Relaxing fun times with family and friends who bring you comfort and joy is medicine to the soul and body. Laughter releases endorphins that recharge your mind and body similar to that of exercise. In short, laughter is good for you.

Laughter is best shared with others. The Bible says we are Christ's body. We are inextricably linked to other believers. We cannot function on our own. Jesus came to restore relationship with the Father and spoke continually of what right relationships look like. You and I cannot fully function at a healthy level without supportive relationships in our life. We need the kind of relationships that help us laugh. As your journey into wholeness continues, find time to laugh. Especially treasure time to laugh with friends and family. Discover your place in the body. They need you too!

Some action points:

- Ask yourself, "Am I making time to laugh and enjoy time with friends?"

- Take a moment to read Psalms 37:3 and 2:4. How does knowing that God laughs affect your understanding of Him?

- Can you remember a time when you saw or sensed God's sense of humor?

Prayer

Lord, thank You that You like to laugh too. Lead me into relationships and situations where I can relax and laugh in and at life.

About the Author

One of Christy Lane's gifts is to create hunger. She desires to take what she's learned and multiply it to as many as she can. Sowing seeds of encouragement and growth is part of her spiritual DNA. She has a Master's degree in Education and owned a retail business for 13 years. She is a former YWAMer, which allowed her to travel to more than eight nations. Christy also directed Sozo at her church in East Texas. She now resides in Redding, CA with her husband Russ, where she is involved with Bethel Healing Rooms, ministry teams, and intercession. Christy is working on her certificate to become a life coach.

www.christykingdomcoaching.com

36288035R00047

Printed in Poland
by Amazon Fulfillment
Poland Sp. z o.o., Wrocław